AFTERLIFE

by

THOMAS JAMES

Crooked Circle Press

Bailey, CO / 2025

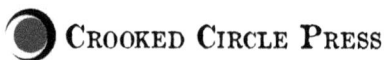

CROOKED CIRCLE PRESS

ISBN: 979-8-9888904-8-5 (Paperback)
ISBN: 979-8-9888904-9-2 (EPUB)

First Edition

www.crookedcirclepress.com
www.thomasjames.me

Contents

Precipice

It feels like possibility and precipice.
It reels like serendipity and fate.
It urges post-apocalyptic genesis.
It verges on an onus to create.

The song in it was first sung as an elegy,
a longing that was whispered through a dirge.
An anthem is emerging from the melody
as candor and determination surge.

The Tao that can be named is not the timeless one.
A vow that's bent and broken is the norm.
These rails belie ambition when all's said and done;
it fails to hold its own against the storm.

The present tension leads us to a period
that some imperfect past did so endow.
The futures laid before us here are myriad.
The sutures are still holding as of now.

Afterlife

My afterlife is never Heaven; rarely is it Hell.
We all decay with time; aside from that, I'm doing well.
My former formal form is not a thing on which to dwell,
but no, momentum can't unring a bell.

Pavlovian, cyclopean, the tolerances bleed.
It's bigger than a Skinner box and smaller than a seed.
It won't respond to wants while there is ever so much need.
I'm awled by its efficiency and speed.

My afterlife is not Nirvana; winds of change yet blow.
I'm riding on the thermals and responding to the flow.
I'm trying to avert my eyes from rough terrain below,
but such systemic change is strange and slow.

Newtonian, but protean, the tides of fate roll in.
A win becomes a loss, and then a loss becomes a win.
The only certainty is that we end and then begin,
and nothing will remain the way it's been.

My afterlife is not the Field of Reeds or perfect Nile,
no bland reward awaiting those who go the extra mile.
A change more qualitative than a subtle shift in style.
No quantitative increase in my smile.

Idealized, unrealized, but that's just how it goes.
The cosmos is built perfectly to keep us on our toes.
It's hard to be content and let resentment decompose,
but when I can, I focus on the pros.

My afterlife is Sheol, where the good and wicked wait,
a hot mess, but suspended in a cryogenic state,
a flight into oblivion that never leaves the gate.
Another day too short and dollar late.

Affirmative alternative where all is as it seems.
There's nothing to be gained from having hopes, or plans, or dreams,
but take it day by day, and slowly shore up all your seams.
Pure gold is not the only thing that gleams.

Last Night

Last night, I found myself too tired to sleep.
I'd counted on more energetic sheep.
My masochistic machinations in a haggard heap,
the kanban boards and spreadsheets softly weep.

Last night, I wrote a checklist I can't cash.
I tagged a host of issues to rehash.
Al dente challenges provide a satisfying gnash,
but heavy eyelids can't escape the lash.

Last night, I pushed tomorrow, but it came;
mid-morning with a modicum of shame.
I burned the midnight oil until fatigue turned down the flame,
but rest remained elusive all the same.

Last night, I settled into gravity.
I set my nerve and muscle fibers free.
I loosed the flashing arrows pointing where I ought to be
and waited for the dark to cover me.

Originally Published in *The Crooked Circle* on Medium on December 27, 2024

Imaginary

He is, himself, (and this is true) his own worst adversary.
He lays upon the lounging chair, as still as statuary.
The traffic sounds berate him, and as always, he is wary.
The flames that are surrounding him are just imaginary.
The flames you see consuming him are all imaginary.

The choices that were made for him were simply arbitrary.
He tried to douse himself in cool and soothing sanctuary
but, sentence after sentence, found himself in solitary.
These flames that are engulfing him are but imaginary.
These bright blue torrid flames are totally imaginary.

He studies every nuance with internal commentary.
He's lost in any room in which he isn't necessary.
He cannot face the thought that he'll be ever ancillary.
The flames that melt his eyes are nothing but imaginary.
The flames that scorch his will are raging and imaginary.

Human Condition

The human condition,
these wars of attrition,
my dicey position,
cacophonous head;
through baked-in aversions,
deflected incursions,
I'm upgrading versions
and beating the spread.

Though vain hope bewitches,
reality twitches;
I tighten my stitches
and bring out my dead.
If earth should stop quaking,
and precedent, breaking,
my heart could stop aching
and soften instead.

Collective

A shard of doubts, a swarm of pangs,
a herd of cruel obscenities.
A card of bouts, a storm of bangs,
a murder of identities.

A school of flaws, a troop of lies,
a colony of scrutiny.
A pool of pause, a loop of sighs,
a self-respect of mutiny.

A cage of fears, a flame of plans,
a deficit of remedies.
A rage of tears, a shame of Dans,
an awkwardness of memories.

A squall of pains, a slough of thoughts,
a sundering of aegises
A crawl of chains, a bluff of oughts,
a hominin of weaknesses.

To Matter

To matter is a matter of survival.
To count can counteract the pointlessness.
If affect can affect a rare revival,
then import is important to success.

The needlestick of need can bleed like seeping.
Fulfilment can feel full like dreamless rest.
At worst, a worthlessness that's still worth keeping;
impertinently pertinent at best.

Absence

Everything you have can yet be taken;
objects, people, sanity, and health.
Just as many faithful are forsaken.
Some who sleep on benches once had wealth.

All is subject to a repossession.
One disaster wipes the slate so clean.
Living is an infinite regression.
God is dead; the universe is mean.

Rights exist if others choose to grant them.
Nature still is red in tooth and claw.
You may wave a flag or sing an anthem.
Nations are constructed out of law.

Sorry, but the cavalry's not coming.
Calvary won't save your dirty soul.
You'll become whatever you're becoming.
See through the illusion of control.

Don't attach yourself to future losses.
Snuff the sense of fairness in your head.
Grin and bear your multitude of crosses.
Pain is a reminder you're not dead.

Impassé

Impassé.
So yesterday.
The obstacle has gone away.

EnMitty.
Pretense set free.
Another way that things could be.

Cur(s)e of hope.
No gyroscope.
No compass needle pushing dope.

Press your lux.
Align your ducks
in random walk and constant flux.

Neverfrozen

Sands of time, the grains are crashing,
wrapped in glass awant of smashing.
Falling earthward, wailing, gnashing;
crystal moments, clumping, clashing.

Breakers whitecap, stormy weather.
Beaching, teaching, rockrose heather.
Bird in hand and bird of feather,
then and now, and altogether.

Sink a stone and skip a season.
Fill a void devoid of reason.
Perfidy, thy name is legion.
Trust is requisite to treason.

Pinned between the wabe and gnomon,
thunderous like fate or omen,
swelling as the open ocean,
everchanging, neverfrozen.

Here and Now

Where and when?
Here and now.
There and then?
Oh, and how!

Tapestry.
Twisted thread.
Tangle me.
Troll the dead.

Futures past
failed to be.
Dice were cast
(not by me).

Overwent.
Undercame.
Reinvent.
Change my name.

Rooster fight.
Chicken run.
Left and write.
Said and done.

Magic beans,
Chia pet.
By all means.
Outsize bet.

Nevermind.
Evermore.
Flying blind.
Losing score.

There and then?
Oh, and how!
Where and when?
Here and now.

Blink

When it's been a week of a day,
and the scars conspire against me,
I wish I could

    Blink.

In the warmth of a hell of a heaven,
where the demons have halos,
I wish I could

    Blink.

After a marathon of a sprint,
when the finish line is electrified,
I wish I could

    Blink.

Where the end of a beginning
hits the middle of an end,
I wish I could

    Blink.

Having been brilliantly foolish,
as the shockwave approaches,
I wish I could

    Blink.

In a particularly thunderous silence,
when even the seconds feel thick,
I wish I could

    Blink.

Under a misspelled spell,
where hex marks the spot,
I wish I could

    Blink.

Under the auspices of my present past,
when I find myself guilty,
I wish I could

Blink.

Pyramid

Climbing Maslow's pyramid
with drastic, reckless speed
is dizzying under ideal conditions,
clambering the steps amid
your ever growing need,
and resting in undignified positions.
Starting as an elder kid
and learning what you need
precludes development of grand ambitions.
Times you would have run and hid
become when you succeed;
the sysadmin has granted write permissions.

Lee

On the verge of a surge in my urge just to be,
I'm afraid I might fade and degrade in the lee.
I am pinned by the wind, and chagrined by the sea,
and the jet stream is set against me.

Here, the breakwater takes all the shake from the brine,
and the shore asks for more while the oracles whine.
I am speaking, and eking, and seeking a sign.
How the lighthouse doth sightlessly shine!

I fell short leaving port, though exhorted to go.
Some will rove past the cove whence I drove through the snow,
standing tall through each squall, never stalling or slow,
but the wise know the sky's bound to blow.

I will venture again where the sentries are blind.
I will sail without fail where the frail cannot find.
I will weep in the deep, but I'll keep this in mind:
there is art in the part left behind.

The Shape I'm In

The shape I'm in is
annular, like haze around the moon.
The shape I'm in is
sinuous like Sunday afternoon.

The shape I'm in is
natural; it bends like laurels do.
The shape I'm in is
convex as the drops of morning dew.

The shape I'm in is
piniform with scales in phalanx rows.
The shape I'm in is
angular; acute at that, god knows.

The shape I'm in is
billowy, like plumes of wildfire smoke.
The shape I'm in is
oblong, like a distance-running joke.

The shape I'm in is
tetrahedral, caltrops everywhere.
The shape I'm in is
blurry when I'm only halfway there.

The shape I'm in is
an ellipse with foci strewn about.
The shape I'm in is
tortuous; the perfect scenic route.

The shape I'm in is
asymptotic, never reaching home.
The shape I'm in is
Brownian; I'm bound to bounce and roam.

The shape I'm in is
just the one that happened to unfold.
The shape I'm in is
overstuffed with stories yet untold.

Morning Breaks

When morning breaks like chains,
the day feels fully fetterless.
I'm holding my own reins,
and work is effortless.

When morning breaks a sweat,
my labors seek a just reward,
where all my needs are met,
and I can sheathe my sword.

When morning breaks the mold,
and I've gone off the only map,
there's nothing left to hold;
the unknowns overlap.

When morning breaks like glass,
and sunbeams shatter on the floor,
the shards of sharpness pass
as kidney stones or war.

When morning breaks my fall,
my long, dark tumble through a night,
another midnight squall
gives way to lucid light.

When morning breaks a spell,
enchantment snaps and sublimates.
A bold and baleful knell,
the slam of iron gates.

When morning breaks like news,
reality is bound to change.
Prepare for shifting views
and learn to rearrange.

When morning breaks my heart,
and it is not repaired by noon,
those tragedies impart
a bitter sort of boon.

Originally Published in *Thomas James Poetry* on Substack on March 11, 2025

The Face in the Mirror

The face in the mirror has aged—
front lines of the wars I have waged.
The trenches where armies engaged
spider the field.
With all that's been said and Verdun,
the shells that have blocked out the sun,
the end has already begun,
landscape unhealed.

The face in the mirror has wept
at damage from secrets well-kept
as instincts and selfish needs slept,
waiting for death.
The floods came to wipe clean the Earth,
a baptism and a rebirth,
still trying to learn what I'm worth,
fighting for breath.

The face in the mirror is new,
defaced by the things I unknew,
abased by the turn of the screw,
whine of the drill.
Disguised by removing a mask,
it's nothing, and all I can ask.
Off camber, but still I'm on task
holding this hill.

The face in the mirror is mine,
a billboard that offers no sign
of how hard I'm pushing toward fine,
ready or not.
An ad that can only subtract,
unpacking a sinister pact
'til legend dissolves into fact;
that's all we've got.

The Will of the Way

Into a headwind and fresh out of chances,
here in the third act, the curtain falls hard.
Steadfast delays with sporadic advances,
spewing soliloquys, splendidly scarred.

How many roads must a man wander idly?
How many times must the cannonballs fly?
Whirlwinds of answers, available widely:
sponsored result or a popular lie?

Seeking the means through eternal regression,
even a stopped clock is right twice a day.
Led by a frivolous lifelong obsession,
learning to trust in the will of the way.

Creature of the Moment

Oh, creature of the moment,
you are perfectly adapted
to a habitat
that's very
nearly
gone.

Oh, product of the present,
specialized and calibrated
by a past in which
you were a
perfect
pawn.

Consider all the vectors,
all the variable factors,
that conspired to form
this life you're
living
now.

If hindsight's 20/20,
retrospect's a funhouse mirror
that distorts the shape
of every
erstwhile
vow.

A cloud's quicksilver lining
can precipitate a flood stage
which can make the sand
beneath your
feet as
fast.

Set out upon the waters
with a raft of craft or scheming,
and the bout of storm
and carry
will not
last.

An end is always looming
in the guise of a beginning
or a twisted plot
that knots the
open
sky.

So shed your skin and lighten,
see your muted colors brighten,
and transcend the need
to ever
wonder
why.

Dusk

In a dusk such as this,
on the shores of abyss,
trying hard to dismiss seismic strife,
as the sun fades to black,
recollections attack,
and the stars start to crackle to life.

When the evening grows dark,
and the contrast more stark
between space and a spark of belief,
it's the ravenous chill
of a death on a hill
that purloins iron will like a thief.

There's a war on for peace,
and the stakes just increase
until heartbeats surcease in good time.
In the still of the night
and the absence of sight,
I abandon my fight to sublime.

'Fore the dawntreaders tread,
time could leave me stone dead
despite falling ahead like I do.
In the houses of light,
each illuminate plight
is a nightmare that might not come true.

Alpenglow

I say the things I need to hear
but hear the words of old.
I fill the holes from yesteryear
with hope too thin to hold.

I see with 20/20 eyes;
please disregard the beam.
I catalog and catalyze
each evanescent dream.

I trace a topographic scar,
a map of where I've been.
I leave my heart and mind ajar
to let the lovelight in.

I radiate the energy
I learned to live without.
I overcome the lethargy
from overwhelm and doubt.

I stride ahead with confidence
in things I cannot know.
I'm on my own recognizance
and bathed in alpenglow.

Originally Published in *Write Under the Moon* on Medium, December 6, 2025

Thanks for reading.
Get a new, exclusive
Thomas James
poem every month!*